You can see thousands of stars on a clear night, but only one star can be seen during the day. It lights up our sky. What is this star?

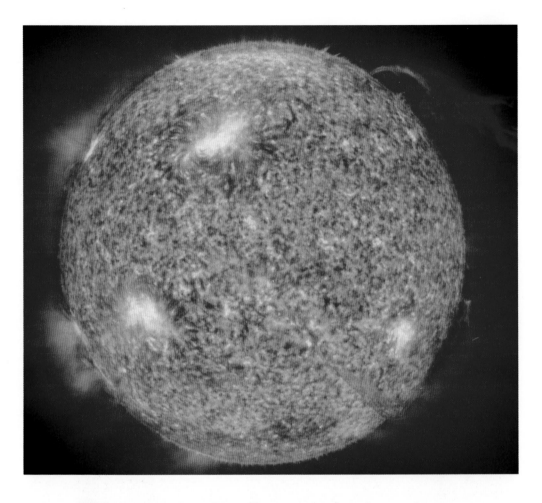

This star is the Sun. It is the closest
star to the Earth. The Earth is our
home planet.

4

The Sun

by Margaret J Goldstein

Lerner Books • London • New York • Minneapolis

First published in the United Kingdom in 2008 by
Lerner Books,
Dalton House,
60 Windsor Avenue,
London SW19 2RR

Website address: www.lernerbooks.co.uk

This edition was updated and edited for UK publication by Discovery Books Ltd., Unit 3, 37 Watling Street, Leintwardine, Shropshire SY7 0LW

Words in **bold type** are explained in a glossary on page 30.

British Library Cataloguing in Publication Data

Goldstein, Margaret J.
  The Sun. - (Our universe)
  1. Sun - Juvenile literature
  I. Title
  523.7

  ISBN-13: 978 1 58013 464 4

The photographs in this book are reproduced with permission from: © Betty Sederquist/Visuals Unlimited, p 3; © NASA, pp 4, 5; © John Sanford, pp 9, 12, 19, 23; © ESA/Tsado/Tom Stack & Associates, pp 11, 25; © Science VU/Visuals Unlimited, p 13; © Charles Newman/Visuals Unlimited, p 15; © A & E Morris/Visuals Unlimited, p 16; © Minneapolis Public Library, Animals p 21; © NOAA/ Tsado/Tom Stack & Associates, p 26; © Jeff Greenberg/Visuals Unlimited, p 27. Cover: NASA.

Printed in China

The Sun is at the centre of the **solar system.** The solar system has nine planets, and the Earth is one of these nine planets.

All of the planets in the solar system travel around the Sun. The Earth is the third planet from the Sun.

THE SOLAR SYSTEM

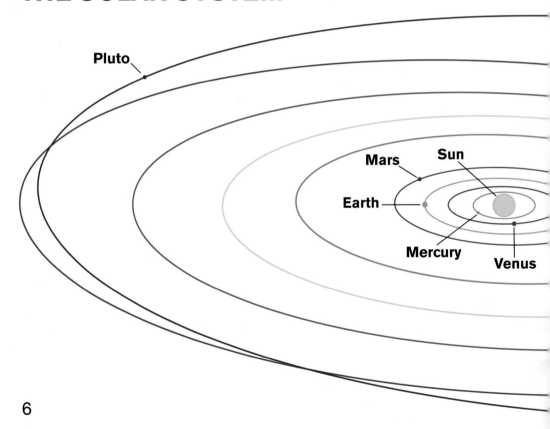

The Sun's heat and light travel out to the planets in the solar system. The planets close to the Sun get the most heat and light. Planets far from the Sun get much less heat and light.

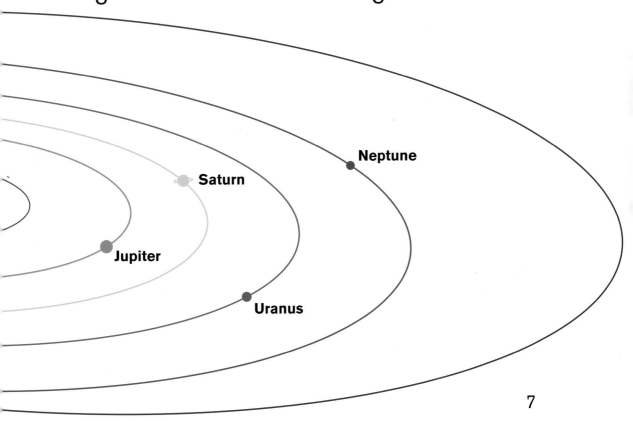

Neptune

Saturn

Jupiter

Uranus

The Sun is much bigger than anything else in the solar system. More than a million planets like the Earth could fit inside the Sun. The Sun is not the biggest or brightest star in space.

The Sun

Earth

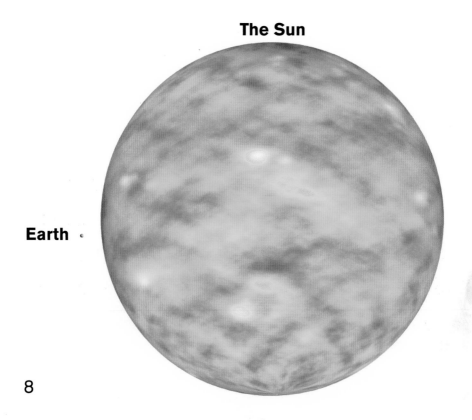

The Sun is a medium-sized star. It is the closest star to the Earth, so it looks bigger and brighter than other stars. Other stars look small because they are very far away.

Like all stars, the Sun is a giant ball of hot gases. It is like a huge furnace. Temperatures deep inside the Sun are millions of degrees above zero. This is much, much hotter than any place on Earth.

The inside of the Sun is called the **core.** Heat from the core travels to the outside of the Sun. The outside of the Sun is called the **surface.** The surface is not as hot as the core, but it is still very hot.

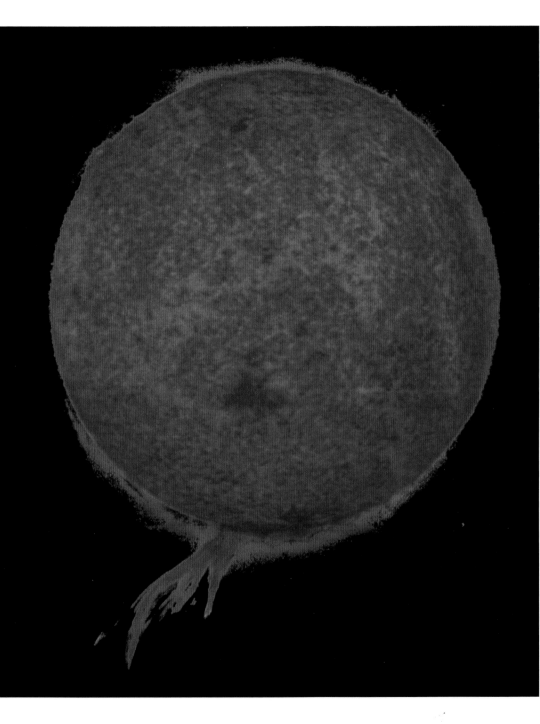

Some places on the surface of the Sun are cooler than other places. These cooler places are called **sunspots.** Sunspots look like small dark patches on the Sun.

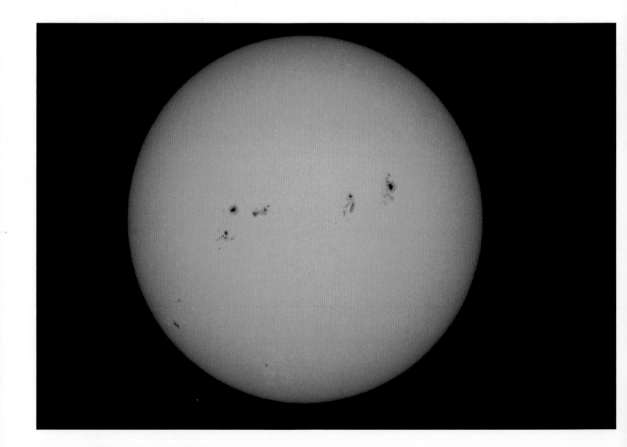

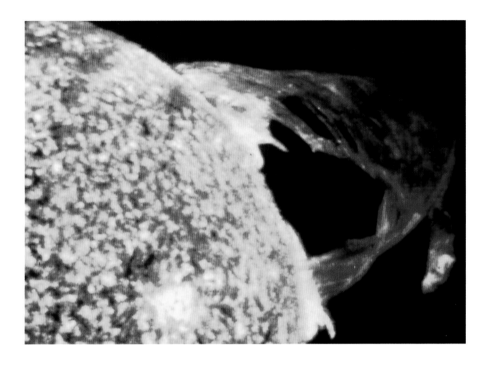

Sometimes glowing gases shoot up
from the surface of the Sun. The gases
make big loops. The Sun also gives off
bursts of light and heat. These bursts
are called **solar flares.**

Streams of tiny **particles** flow from the Sun. These particles are called the **solar wind**. Blasts of the solar wind sometimes reach the Earth.

You cannot see or feel the solar wind, but it can cause the sky on Earth to glow at night. This glowing light is called an **aurora.** Auroras happen only in the far northern and southern parts of the Earth.

The Sun lights up our sky during the day. The Sun seems to rise in the sky in the morning and sink again at night. The Sun looks like it is moving because the Earth is always spinning.

DAY AND NIGHT

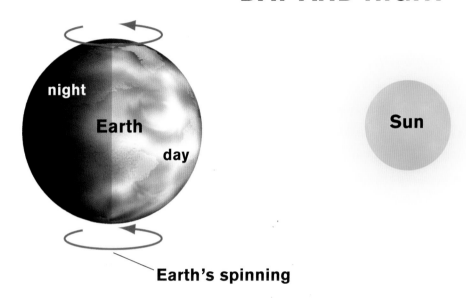

The Earth spins around. The spinning gives us day and night. In the morning, your side of the Earth spins to face the Sun. In the evening, your side of the Earth spins back away from the Sun.

Sometimes the Moon seems to cover up the Sun. The Moon circles the Earth. As the Moon travels, it sometimes moves between the Earth and the Sun. Then the Moon blocks the Sun's light for a few minutes. On parts of the Earth, the sky grows dark. This event is called a **solar eclipse.**

The Sun is very important to the Earth.
The Sun warms the land and the
oceans on our planet. Sunlight helps
keep people, plants and animals warm,
too.

Sunlight also helps plants grow.
People and animals need plants for
food. Without the Sun, there would be
no food to eat. There would be no life
on Earth.

Humans have wondered about the Sun for thousands of years. But people cannot look right at the Sun for very long. The Sun's bright light is too strong.

Astronomers are people who study outer space. Astronomers use special telescopes to look at the Sun. These telescopes help astronomers study the Sun without harming their eyes.

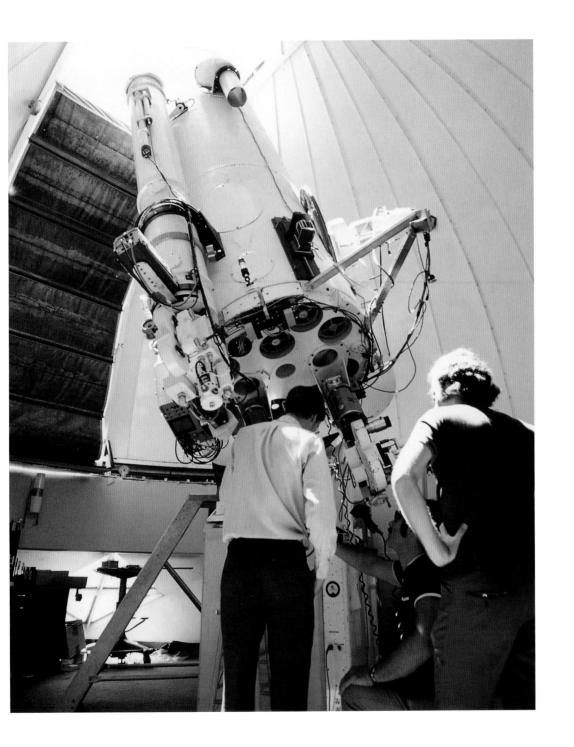

Astronauts have studied the Sun. Astronauts are people who travel from the Earth to space. In the 1970s, astronauts studied the Sun from a space station called *Skylab.*

Spacecraft without astronauts have studied the Sun, too. The spacecraft carried machines that measured the Sun's heat and light. They also carried cameras that took pictures of the Sun.

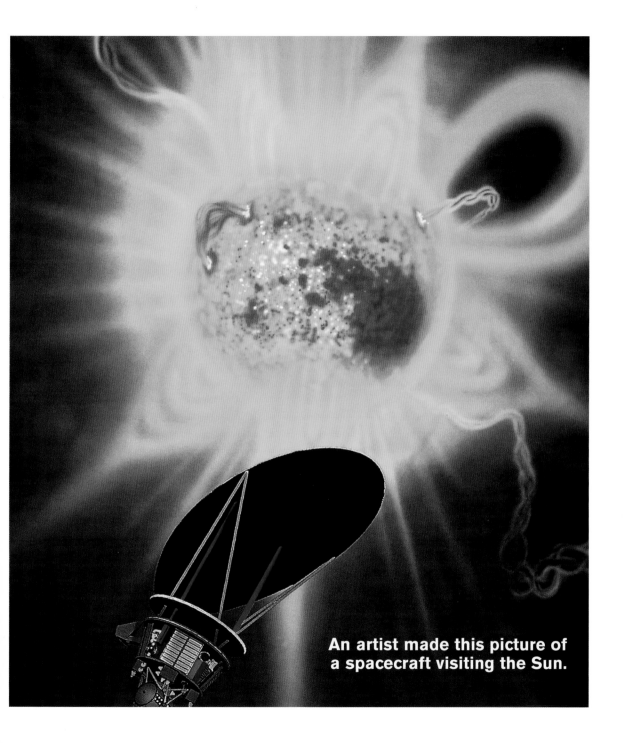

An artist made this picture of a spacecraft visiting the Sun.

A spacecraft called *Genesis* left Earth in 2001. Its aim was to study solar wind. *Genesis* crash landed on its return to Earth in 2004, but scientists were still able to get information from it.

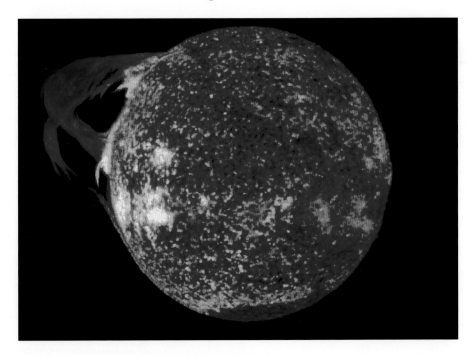

You can see the Sun shine. You can feel its heat on your skin. Ask your own questions about the Sun. Then try to find the answers.

Facts about the Sun

- The Sun is about 150,000,000 km (93,000,000 miles) from the Earth.

- The Sun is 58,000,000 km (36,000,000 miles) from Mercury, the innermost planet in the solar system and 5,900,100,000 km (3,666,000,000 miles) from Pluto, the outermost planet.

- The Sun's diameter (distance across) is 1,400,000 km (864,000 miles).

- The average temperature of the Sun's core is (15,000,000°C)

- The average temperature of the Sun's surface is 5,500°C.

- The Sun is made mostly of hydrogen and helium, but at least 70 other gases are also part of the Sun.

- Some stars are 1,000 times wider than the Sun.

- The Sun is at least 4.5 billion years old.

- The Sun is brighter than all the lightbulbs on Earth put together.

- The Sun will keep shining for about another 5 billion years.

- The Sun is much too hot for any person to stand on it. A human would burn up long before reaching the Sun.

- The Sun has strong gravity, the force that pulls you towards the ground. If you weighed 35 kilograms on Earth, you would weigh 900 kilograms on the Sun!

- At least a dozen spacecraft are studying the Sun or the effects of the Sun on the Earth.

Glossary

astronauts: people who travel to outer space

astronomers: people who study outer space

aurora: coloured lights that glow in the sky in far northern and southern parts of the Earth

core: the centre of the Sun

particles: tiny bits of matter

solar eclipse: when the Moon blocks out the Sun's light

solar flares: bursts of heat and light that shoot up from the Sun

solar system: the Sun and the planets, moons and other objects that travel around it

solar wind: tiny particles that flow from the Sun

surface: the outer layer of an object

sunspots: dark patches on the Sun's surface

Learn More about the Sun

Books

Graham, Ian. *The Sun* (Discovering Space) Franklin Watts Ltd, 2007.

Whitehouse, Patricia. *The Sun* (Space Explorer) Heinemann Library, 2004.

Websites

Solar System Exploration: The Sun
http://solarsystem.nasa.gov/features/planets/sun/sun.html
Detailed information from the National Aeronautics and Space Administration (NASA) about the Sun, with good links to other helpful websites.

The Space Place
http://spaceplace.jpl.nasa.gov
An astronomy website for kids developed by NASA's Jet Propulsion Laboratory.

BBC Science and Nature: Space
http://www.bbc.co.uk/science/space/
This website has loads of information about space and the Sun.

Index

First published in the United States of America in 2003
Text copyright © 2003 by Margaret J Goldstein